Original title:
Ice Shadows

Copyright © 2024 Swan Charm
All rights reserved.

Author: Paula Raudsepp
ISBN HARDBACK: 978-9916-79-663-4
ISBN PAPERBACK: 978-9916-79-664-1
ISBN EBOOK: 978-9916-79-665-8

Resplendent Layers of Ice

Crystals glisten in the pale light,
Reflecting dreams in a frozen sight.
Each layer whispers of winter's grace,
Nature's art, a timeless embrace.

Fragile beauty shrouded in white,
A symphony born of the frosty night.
Every breath clouds in the air,
Mirrored moments, both rare and fair.

Beneath the surface, secrets lie,
Waiting for spring's warm goodbye.
Nature's palette, soft and bright,
Under the moon, a magical sight.

The world holds its breath in the chill,
Time seems to pause, a perfect thrill.
Silent shadows dance in the breeze,
Carved in ice, with effortless ease.

As winter wanes, the layers fade,
A promise of warmth in sunlight laid.
Yet in this cold, memories remain,
Resplendent layers that still entertain.

Serenade in the Glittering Cold

Under the stars, the night unfolds,
A serenade in whispers untold.
Gentle snowflakes twirl and sway,
In the glittering cold, they softly play.

Each flake a note of winter's song,
Melodies sweet, where dreams belong.
Softly they land, a delicate kiss,
In silence wrapped, pure winter bliss.

The moonlight dances on icy streams,
Chasing shadows, weaving dreams.
In this embrace, the world stands still,
Time cherishes each fleeting thrill.

A blanket of white, a canvas wide,
Nature's brilliance, unconfined pride.
With each breath, we gather the night,
In this serenade, our hearts take flight.

So let us wander through worlds unmade,
In the glittering cold, our fears allayed.
For in this beauty, we find our way,
A serenade for a perfect day.

Ephemeral Traces

In the morning light,
Shadows softly fade,
Memories take flight,
Time cannot be stayed.

Marks upon the sand,
Waves wash them away,
Life's a fleeting hand,
Turning night to day.

Glimpse of laughter shared,
Echoes in the breeze,
Moments unprepared,
Whispers through the trees.

Each glance a soft sigh,
Unraveled by the hour,
Fleeting dreams a lie,
Soft petals from a flower.

In the dusk we part,
Yet still I will keep,
The traces of heart,
In memories deep.

Glimmers in the Frost

Morning's breath so crisp,
Glimmers dance and play,
Nature's crystal lisp,
In the light of day.

Frost upon the leaves,
Whispers quick and light,
A secret that weaves,
Glimmers into sight.

Each step leaves a mark,
In the icy ground,
A fleeting spark,
In silence profound.

Days in cold embrace,
Glints of silver hue,
Nature's gentle grace,
Awakes me anew.

As the sun ascends,
I watch the frost fade,
Beauty never ends,
In the light cascades.

Whispers Beneath the Glaze

Beneath the shining sheen,
Stories softly dwell,
In reflections keen,
Unraveling their spell.

Glass around me speaks,
Voices from the past,
In quiet mystiques,
Whispers here amassed.

Every touch reveals,
Layers long concealed,
Tenderness it heals,
In the warmth revealed.

Through the frozen night,
Glimmers fight to stay,
A dance of pure light,
Keeping dark at bay.

In the dawn I hear,
Echoes feel so clear,
Whispers drawing near,
Bringing love and cheer.

Frosted Echoes

Underneath the stars,
Frosted echoes gleam,
Whispering the scars,
Of an old, lost dream.

Silent in the night,
Each breath brings a chill,
Yet the world feels right,
With a peace that stills.

Moonlight paints the ground,
Silver laced and bright,
Nature's magic found,
In the cloak of night.

As the dawn appears,
Frost begins to fade,
Echoes turn to cheers,
In soft light displayed.

Hold the moments tight,
In frosted embrace,
Every fleeting sight,
Leaves a loving trace.

Sighs Beneath the Frost

In a silent world of white,
Whispers echo through the night.
Nature breathes a frozen sigh,
Underneath the pale, vast sky.

Crystals cradle every thought,
Teardrops of the cold are caught.
Each breath lingers, soft and slow,
As winter's chill begins to grow.

Glistening on the branches bare,
Timeless secrets fill the air.
A tranquil hush, a sacred pause,
Frosted dreams in nature's laws.

The Glistening Trace of Time

Sparkling wings in the winter light,
Hold the stories of the night.
Each flake a memory, pure and bright,
In the silence, they take flight.

Footprints trail in the morning snow,
Showing where the heart did go.
A path unravels, lost yet clear,
In the glistening, we draw near.

Time dances lightly, shimmers the soul,
Framed by frost, it makes us whole.
Moments captured, fleeting grace,
In each glimmer, we find our place.

Flickers of Cold Radiance

Stars twinkle in the frost-laden air,
Each flicker whispers, dreams to share.
Underneath the icy dome,
We wander softly, far from home.

Cold radiance burns so bright,
Illuminating the heart's quiet fight.
Each breath a visible sign,
Of warmth hidden deep divine.

Glistening paths of light ignite,
Guiding spirits through the night.
Amidst the cold, we feel the spark,
Finding joy within the dark.

Secrets Woven in Frost

Beneath the patterns laid in white,
Secrets whisper, soft and light.
Frosted tales of yesteryear,
Echo gently, drawing near.

Each crystal holds a quiet song,
Of where we've belonged all along.
Woven into the fabric, vast,
Are the memories that will last.

Nature scribes its love in ice,
A fleeting moment, rich and nice.
Silent stories in the dawn,
Frosted beauty lingers on.

Reflections of a Chilled Heart

In the stillness, silence lies,
Frosty breath beneath clear skies.
A heart encased in icy dreams,
Echoing softly, or so it seems.

Memories drift like leaves in air,
Spirits whisper, lost in despair.
Through frosted panes, the world recedes,
Alone with thoughts, where darkness breeds.

Shadows dance in the silver light,
Fragments sparkle, dimmed by night.
Each heartbeat echoes, cold and stark,
Carving paths through memories dark.

Ghosts of joy now wrapped in chill,
Time stands still, yet dreams instill.
Silence wraps the heart so tight,
Bound in echoes of lost light.

The Glitter of Frozen Time

Snowflakes tumble, a gentle sigh,
Each one whispers, drifting by.
Glistening trails on twilight's skin,
A frozen world, where dreams begin.

Icicles gleam like shards of glass,
Silent sentinels as people pass.
Fleeting moments, caught mid-air,
Captured whispers of winter's prayer.

A timeline etched in crystal fair,
Memories dance in the cool, crisp air.
Stars reflect on surfaces bright,
Holding secrets of the night.

Each frost-kissed branch tells stories old,
Veils of winter, shimmering gold.
Time suspends in a breathless trance,
Inviting hearts to join the dance.

Ethereal Layers of Cold

In the quiet, layers unfold,
Soft caresses, painfully bold.
A tapestry of frost and glaze,
Woven whispers in a frozen haze.

Frosted petals, a delicate weave,
Nature sings, yet bids us grieve.
Frozen echoes of voices past,
Carving paths that forever last.

Beneath the surface, warmth still stirs,
Hopes entwined in winter's blurs.
Encased in beauty, silence reigns,
From frozen roots, life still gains.

A heart encased in layers thick,
Waiting for the sun's soft flick.
When warmth returns to melt the snow,
Will these hidden feelings show?

Glinting Shimmers in the Gloom

In shadowed corners, light may seep,
Glimmers fleeting, secrets keep.
Each twinkle whispers tales unknown,
In the dark, where dreams have grown.

Faint silhouettes in night's embrace,
A haunting dance, a timeless grace.
Stars flicker shyly, dim but true,
Fighting darkness with their view.

Cold caress of the evening breeze,
Murmurs drift through swaying trees.
In every shiver, a story bends,
In glinting shimmers, time transcends.

Through veils of night, the heart still gleams,
Holding fast to fragile dreams.
With every breath, the shadows sigh,
A promise kept beneath the sky.

Frostbite Reveries

Morning mist wraps soft and white,
Children's laughter, pure delight.
Winter's chill bites with a grace,
In frozen worlds, we find our place.

Icicles hang, sharp and bright,
Whispers dance in the pale moonlight.
Footsteps crunch on powdered snow,
In dreams of warmth, our hopes do grow.

Through the woods, a silent glide,
Nature's beauty, our hearts bide.
Frosted branches, glimmering lace,
In the stillness, we find our space.

Frozen lakes, a crystal mirror,
As winter's tune finds its clearer.
Timeless moments, fleeting fast,
In frosty dreams, forever cast.

Night descends, stars gleam above,
Cold embraces, a touch of love.
In this realm of chill and fear,
Frostbite whispers, "We are here."

Shadows of the Glinting Moon

Beneath the silver's gentle hue,
Whispers flow, soft and true.
Shadows dance on the forest floor,
Secrets held forevermore.

Night unfolds with velvet grace,
Moonlight weaves, a tender lace.
Crickets sing their lullaby,
Echoes fade as dreams drift by.

Stars flicker in a vast embrace,
Guiding wanderers through the space.
Cool breeze carries ancient tales,
Of loves lost and whispered wails.

Cloaked in darkness, spirits soar,
In the quiet, we explore.
Underneath the watchful eye,
In shadows deep, we learn to fly.

With each breath of the night's sweet air,
We find solace, free of care.
In the stillness, hearts attune,
To the shadows of the glinting moon.

Ethereal Frost

Dewdrops sparkle, mornings bright,
In the dawn, a breathtaking sight.
Ethereal frost clings to the ground,
In this hush, peace is found.

Breath hangs heavy, a whispering ghost,
Nature's beauty, we cherish most.
Branches taste the cold embrace,
Life, in slumber, finds its place.

Winds carry tales from times of yore,
Of lullabies and open doors.
Underneath the blanket pale,
Silent wishes, hearts set sail.

Frosty petals, delicate and frail,
In winter's grasp, they softly pale.
Yet in their beauty, strength resides,
As seasons change, and time abides.

In quiet corners of our dreams,
Ethereal frost whispers and gleams.
With each glint of winter's art,
Nature's magic enchants the heart.

Nature's Silent Artistry

Sunrise spills its golden light,
Painting hills in hues so bright.
Each dawn blooms with endless grace,
Nature's touch in every space.

Gentle streams, a soothing tune,
Reflecting skies of vibrant June.
Leaves that rustle, whispers low,
Tell of secrets that they know.

Mountains rise, majestic, bold,
Guardians of the stories told.
Through the valleys, winds do weave,
Crafting moments we believe.

Flora dances, colors sway,
In this timeless grand ballet.
Nature's canvas, vast and free,
Masterpiece for all to see.

As day fades into twilight's hold,
Magic lingers, purest gold.
Life unfurls in silent art,
Capturing beauty in the heart.

Encrypted in Snowflakes

Each flake a whisper, soft and light,
Dancing through the cold, silent night.
Patterns unfold, secrets they keep,
Nature's own message, buried deep.

In a world of white, they drift and twirl,
A fleeting moment, an icy swirl.
Stories of winter, they tell and share,
Magic in air, we pause and stare.

With every touch, a chill we find,
Connecting hearts, both kind and blind.
As they melt away, dreams take flight,
Perfectly formed in the fading light.

Falling like dreams, they blanket the earth,
Whispers of peace, a moment of mirth.
In this serene, frozen ballet,
Nature's soft sigh at the end of day.

The Crystal Veil of Night

A curtain of stars hangs low and near,
Whispers of secrets for those who hear.
Underneath the moon's gentle gaze,
The world transformed in a silvery haze.

Crystals of ice on branches sway,
Shimmering softly, they fade away.
In the stillness, a breath is caught,
Moments of magic, forever sought.

The silence deep, as shadows creep,
Wrapped in dreams, the night we keep.
Under the veil where mysteries dwell,
A hush in the heart, a spell to compel.

With every blink, the stars reply,
Echoes of wishes that dare to fly.
In night's embrace, we find our way,
Guided by light, till the break of day.

Shadows Beneath a Winter's Moon

Cold winds whisper through barren trees,
Casting soft shadows with cold, cruel ease.
The moon, a beacon, bright and round,
Illuminating dreams on the frozen ground.

Footprints linger in the silver glow,
Memories linger in the depths below.
Each shadow holds a story untold,
Of love and loss, of brave and bold.

The night air dances, crisp and clear,
Every heartbeat, a tale we hear.
The moon watches over, serene yet wild,
An ancient witness, nature's child.

In the stillness, we find our place,
Under the stars, in night's warm embrace.
Together we wander, together we roam,
In the shadows of winter, we find our home.

Glacial Whispers

Quietly gliding, the icebergs flow,
Secrets encoded in frost and snow.
Each crack and creak, a tale to share,
Whispers of time, floating in air.

In the stillness, vast and wide,
The ocean glimmers, the glaciers glide.
Ancient voices echo from below,
Memory frozen in the ebb and flow.

Above, the skies breathe in dark hues,
The horizon melts with the midnight blues.
Nature's own canvas, bold and bright,
Glacial whispers echo through the night.

As dawn breaks through, the ice will part,
Revealing the wonders that stir the heart.
Frozen tales of ages gone by,
In glacial whispers, we learn to fly.

The Hushed Landscape

In twilight's cloak, the whispers sigh,
Where shadows stretch 'neath a dusky sky.
The trees stand tall, their secrets pure,
Embracing calm, forever sure.

The river flows with a soft hum,
Reflecting dreams where stillness comes.
Mountains guard the silent vale,
In their embrace, no fears prevail.

The breeze carries tales of old,
Of stories hushed that need not be told.
Each rustling leaf, a gentle plea,
For peace within this tranquil sea.

Stars emerge, the night ignites,
Shimmering softly, casting lights.
In this space, the heart will dance,
Lost in nature's sweet romance.

As dawn arises, hues unfold,
An artist's brush with colors bold.
The landscape breathes a sigh of grace,
In the stillness, we find our place.

Silvery Ghosts

In the moonlight, shadows creep,
Silvery ghosts, their secrets keep.
Dancing lightly on the breeze,
In whispered tones, they aim to please.

Through ancient woods, they softly glide,
On haunting paths where dreams reside.
Beneath the stars, they twirl and weave,
A tapestry of night to believe.

Eyes aglow, they shimmer bright,
Casting spells in the twilight.
With every step, a story blooms,
In the silence, the magic looms.

Echoes of laughter, a distant past,
These fleeting forms will never last.
Yet in their presence, spirits soar,
In the stillness, forevermore.

As dawn approaches, they fade away,
Leaving memories of their play.
In the light, we find our way,
With dreams infused in night's bouquet.

Secrets Beneath the Frost

Beneath the frost, the earth sleeps tight,
Guarding wonders from the light.
In crystalline layers, stories rest,
Nature's secrets, softly dressed.

A whispering chill fills the air,
Of hidden worlds, beyond compare.
Gentle patterns, like lace unfold,
The frost reveals what time has told.

Roots entwined in quiet grace,
Woven tales in a still embrace.
Every flake a mystery,
Carved in silence, meant to be.

When sunlight kisses the icy ground,
A symphony of colors found.
Awakening life from winter's hold,
As secrets thaw, they shall be told.

In this dance of cold and warm,
Nature's cycle takes its form.
With each thaw, a chance reborn,
In whispers shared with every dawn.

Crystalized Silence

In the stillness, crystals gleam,
Caught in a delicate dream.
Fractured light, a prism's hue,
Whispers soft, a tranquil view.

Silence reigns within this space,
Embracing peace, a warm embrace.
Every breath, a gentle pause,
Nature's beauty, worthy applause.

Snowflakes fall like whispered sighs,
Softly drifting from the skies.
Adorned in white, the world transforms,
A canvas pure where quiet warms.

In this crystalized expanse,
Time slows down, we find our chance.
To listen deep, to feel the song,
In silence where we all belong.

As echoes fade and shadows blend,
We find the peace that knows no end.
In frozen stillness, hearts will rise,
A symphony beneath the skies.

Faded Footprints in the Snow

In the hush of winter's breath,
Footprints fade, a silent death.
Memories lost in icy chill,
Nature's canvas, cold and still.

Whispers echo through the trees,
Carried softly by the breeze.
Each mark tells a story true,
Of journeys made and paths anew.

Dancing flakes fall, soft and light,
Veiling tracks from our last flight.
With every step, a tale erased,
In frosted realms, our steps misplaced.

Time drifts on in quiet grace,
Leaving behind a ghostly trace.
A fleeting dance in winter's grasp,
Faded footprints, memories clasped.

Yet in the gleam of morning's sun,
A hint of warmth, a new day begun.
Footprints lost may still remain,
In the heart, the love, the pain.

Flickering Lights in the Winter Dark

In the depths of wintry night,
Flickering lights bring warmth and light.
Candles glow with soft embrace,
Illuminating every space.

Shadows dance upon the walls,
Whispers echo through the halls.
Each flicker tells a story bright,
Of hopes rekindled in the night.

The chill outside, a biting air,
Inside we gather, free from care.
Hot cocoa warms our weary souls,
As laughter weaves and brightly rolls.

Frosted windows, sparkling views,
Hold secrets wrapped in soft hues.
The world outside, a frosty dream,
While we bask in the hearth's gentle beam.

In this moment, time stands still,
Captured hearts, with love we fill.
Flickering lights, in winter dark,
A cozy warmth, a cherished spark.

Facets of Frigid Beauty

Glittering ice on branches sway,
Facets of beauty on display.
Crystals dance in the morning light,
Nature's art, a pure delight.

Snowflakes fall, each unique design,
Delicate whispers, oh so fine.
A world transformed in silvery lace,
Every corner, a gentle grace.

Footsteps crunch on the frozen ground,
Echoes of silence, a soothing sound.
In the cold, we find our peace,
Nature's hold that does not cease.

Riverbanks dressed in frosty sheen,
Reflecting skies of vibrant green.
Facets of winter's purest heart,
Crafted slowly, a work of art.

With each breath, the world stands still,
Caught in magic, time to fill.
Frigid beauty, strong and pure,
In frozen moments, we endure.

The Illusion of Frozen Time

In the stillness of a winter's night,
Time stands still, a wondrous sight.
Snowflakes drift in the moon's soft glow,
Casting spells that ebb and flow.

The clock ticks slow in this icy realm,
Nature's hands upon the helm.
Each moment stretches, a breath so deep,
In tranquil silence, we softly seep.

Frosted branches, delicate lace,
Hold memories in their cold embrace.
Ghostly echoes of laughter past,
In frozen time, they hold us fast.

Stars above, like diamonds gleam,
Time suspended, like a dream.
We wander through this blissful haze,
In winter's grip, we find our ways.

Yet as dawn breaks with golden hue,
The illusion fades, and we start anew.
Frozen time with its tranquil chime,
Leaves us yearning for more, sublime.

Chilling Reflections

In the quiet night, shadows creep,
Whispers echo, secrets deep.
Moonlight dances on the shore,
Crickets sing as thoughts explore.

Rippling waters, glass so clear,
Mirrored dreams that draw me near.
A chill wraps round like an embrace,
Time stands still in this sacred space.

Stars above, they twinkle bright,
Guiding lost souls in the night.
Flickering flames of hope ignite,
In chilling reflections, hearts take flight.

Waves of memories crash and break,
Tides of silence softly wake.
Each ripple holds a story true,
Revealing paths that I once knew.

So I linger by the lake,
In dreams of what the dawn may make.
Nature's pulse a steady song,
In chilling reflections, I belong.

Crystalline Dreams

In the stillness of the night,
Stars blush with a shimmering light.
Crystals glisten on icy trees,
Nature's art, a solemn tease.

Snowflakes whisper as they fall,
Each one different, nature's call.
Shimmering paths where silence lies,
Beneath the vast and open skies.

A frozen world, serene and bright,
Dancing shadows in soft moonlight.
Dreams are cast in shapes so rare,
In crystalline beauty, we lay bare.

Time dissolves in frosty air,
Moments linger, stripped of care.
With every breath, the magic beams,
Awakening the heart with dreams.

So I wander through this land,
With crystalline dreams, a gentle hand.
Nature's wonders, pure and free,
In the stillness, I find me.

Veil of Winter's Sigh

A blanket soft of white and cold,
Covers secrets long untold.
In the hush of winter's grace,
Time stands still in silent space.

Trees wear coats of frosted lace,
Nature's breath, a gentle trace.
The world transformed, so calm, so bright,
Veil of winter cloaks the night.

Footsteps crunch on snow so pure,
In this quiet, hearts endure.
While whispers of the past take flight,
Dreams awaken with the light.

Frosty windows, tales unfold,
Of warmth and love, both brave and bold.
Each moment caught in winter's sigh,
A frozen tear, a gentle cry.

So I wander through this dream,
In the chill, the world redeems.
Veil of winter's tender kiss,
In its grasp, I find my bliss.

Silent Glaciers

In the distance, mountains stand,
Guardians of a frozen land.
Glaciers whisper, tales of old,
Stories woven in ice and cold.

Crisp air carries echoes clear,
Nature's voice for those who hear.
Silent giants, ever grand,
Breathing softly, hand in hand.

Time moves slow, each pulse a beat,
In their shadows, hearts find heat.
Melting memories shape the flow,
Silent glaciers, vast and slow.

A sparkle hints at life's embrace,
Every crevice holds a trace.
With every step, the earth endears,
Through silent glaciers, we face fears.

So I stand at nature's gate,
Awed by beauty, still, sedate.
In the silence, find the key,
Silent glaciers, boundless sea.

Wraiths of the Frozen Realm

In shadows deep where silence dwells,
The wraiths emerge, their whispers swell.
They dance upon the icy breath,
A haunting song of life and death.

With ghostly forms, they weave through snow,
In twilight's grasp, they ebb and flow.
Their eyes like stars, a distant glow,
In realms where time has ceased to grow.

The frozen winds, they bear their cries,
An echo of the ancient skies.
Through the frost, their secrets rise,
In silver mist where darkness lies.

Yet in their wake, a chill bestows,
The whispered tales of long-lost throes.
Through fields of white where sorrow flows,
Their fleeting sorrow gently grows.

Entwined in tales of icy night,
The wraiths embrace the pale moonlight.
In every flake, a memory bright,
Of love once lost, now out of sight.

Serene Shimmers

Beneath the stars, the night unfolds,
A quilt of dreams, in silence told.
Soft beams cascade like gentle streams,
In icy realms, where starlight gleams.

The world adorned in crystal lace,
A tranquil dive, a swift embrace.
Each flake that falls, a fleeting kiss,
A moment wrapped in quiet bliss.

The stillness reigns, the heart does soar,
In whispering winds, we yearn for more.
The shimmered paths that lead us home,
In frosty woods where spirits roam.

With every breath, a magic weaves,
A tapestry of frost and leaves.
Embraced by peace, the world we hold,
In dreams of silver and threads of gold.

Here in the quiet, dreams take flight,
Upon the frozen canvas bright.
In serene shimmers, life we find,
A dance of joy that binds mankind.

Winter's Embrace

The winter's breath, a soft caress,
In white draped fields, we feel the stress.
Yet in the chill, a warmth unfolds,
A comfort found as day grows old.

With every flake, a lullaby,
The world adorned beneath the sky.
In winter's arms, we find our peace,
A gentle hush, a sweet release.

While shadows stretch as daylight wanes,
The silent strength in cold remains.
Through frosted paths, we dare to tread,
In winter's grip, our dreams are fed.

The world a canvas, white and pure,
In every moment, we endure.
Through bitter winds, love's fire ignites,
In winter's embrace, our hearts take flight.

As night descends, the stars appear,
In winter's grasp, we draw them near.
Together wrapped in peace we find,
A solace shared, two souls entwined.

Mirror of the North

The mirror glimmers, seas of white,
Reflecting dreams in soft twilight.
In icy shards, the world unfolds,
A story whispered, yet untold.

Mountains rise like ancient guards,
In silence strong, they hold their cards.
The mirror dances with the light,
A symphony of day and night.

Each ripple forms a tale once spun,
In frozen waves, the past outrun.
The echoes of a fading time,
In shimmering hues, a silent rhyme.

The northern lights embrace the dusk,
In colors weaves a fragrant musk.
With every glance, the heart does soar,
Reflecting hopes we can't ignore.

Beneath the gaze of endless skies,
The mirror shows where beauty lies.
In every glance, a promise gleams,
The mirror holds our deepest dreams.

The Stillness Beneath

In quiet depths where shadows creep,
The echoes of the earth's soft breath,
A world where secrets gently sleep,
And whispers linger, far from death.

Through layers thick, with time's embrace,
The waters mirror skies of gray,
Each ripple hints of hidden grace,
As silence weaves the night and day.

Roots entwined in ancient lore,
The past unfolds with each still tide,
Where memories like ghosts restore,
The tales of life no longer hide.

Beneath the calm, a thrum remains,
A pulse that beats in muted hue,
In stillness, beauty often reigns,
And life persists in shades of blue.

Here in the depths, the heart can learn,
To find the peace that silence brings,
In stillness, vast, we all return,
To hear the song the stillness sings.

Glacial Veils

Beneath the chill of ice and stone,
The beauty hides in frozen grace,
A world untouched, where none have grown,
Wrapped tight in winter's soft embrace.

In twilight's glow, the blue unfolds,
Translucent glimpses of the past,
A tapestry of stories told,
In silence caught, a spell is cast.

The air is crisp, the heavens clear,
A breath that cuts through veil of frost,
And in the stillness, one can hear,
The echoes of what once was lost.

With every shard of glacial light,
A prism's dance through shadows fleeting,
Each crystal shines, refracting bright,
In nature's art, forever meeting.

The silent glaciers guard their fate,
In depths where secrets make their home,
And through the years, they patiently wait,
For spring to wake their ancient poem.

Frigid Reflections

Upon the lake, the ice is deep,
A mirror held to winter's soul,
Where frozen dreams in silence sleep,
And echoes chant a haunting toll.

The sky above, a muted hue,
With wisps of clouds that drift apart,
Beneath the glaze, the world is new,
Yet still holds fast to winter's heart.

Each glimmer speaks of times once bright,
Where laughter danced upon the shore,
In frigid frames, we find our light,
Reflecting all we've known before.

The stillness breathes, a bitter breeze,
With whispers carried through the pines,
In nature's realm, the mind finds ease,
As frigid sounds become divine.

Through winter's lens, we take a chance,
To see the light that stirs within,
In frigid depths, our hearts still glance,
At warm reflections where we've been.

Translucent Histories

In layers past, the stories flow,
Translucent threads that weave and bind,
A tapestry of ebb and glow,
Where whispers linger, intertwined.

Each shadow cast, a ghostly hue,
Reflects the lives that shaped the land,
Through ages lost, yet still so true,
In grains of sand, the past has spanned.

The heartbeats echo through the stone,
In every mark, a tale unfolds,
Of those who walked, who stood alone,
And in their steps, the future molds.

A prism shines where light once played,
Through stained glass windows of our minds,
In histories where hope cascades,
The lessons learned in gentle winds.

So let us turn the pages slow,
To find the grace in what's been cast,
In translucent tales of long ago,
The bonds of time that hold us fast.

Whispers of the Abyss

In the depth of night so deep,
The silent secrets start to creep.
Voices echo through the gloom,
Calling forth from shadowed tombs.

Dark waters churn with ancient tales,
Of sunken ships and ghostly sails.
Each whisper carries lost despair,
A haunting chant hangs in the air.

Beneath the waves where light won't reach,
The stories of the deep ones teach.
A world where silence reigns supreme,
In depths where we no longer dream.

Echoes of a time long past,
Fading fast, a shadow cast.
Yet still they murmur, still they sigh,
In the abyss where darkness lies.

With every wave, the secrets tread,
In currents swirling tales long dead.
The whispers dance in moonlit foam,
A serenade to the sea's cold home.

Frostbound Visions

Beneath the stars, the frost takes flight,
A shimmering realm of silvered light.
Frozen dreams, where crystals bloom,
Awaken softly in the gloom.

The silence holds a magic spell,
In icy woods, so still, so well.
Whispers ride on the winter breeze,
Carrying tales among the trees.

Each breath is mist, a fleeting trace,
In this enchanted, tranquil space.
Skies painted in a violet hue,
Cloaked in frost, the world feels new.

Moonlit paths through crystals pave,
A vision born from nature's brave.
Secrets dwell in frozen streams,
In this quiet land of dreams.

Footprints echo soft and low,
In the land where minutes slow.
Frostbound visions hold us tight,
Through the long and silent night.

Labyrinth of the Frost

In the maze where the cold winds bite,
A labyrinth veiled in shimmering light.
Each turn leads to wonders strange,
As frozen paths begin to change.

Snowflakes swirl like whispers lost,
In this land where warmth is tossed.
Echoes call from deep within,
A hidden truth, a darkened sin.

Icicles dangle like forgotten dreams,
Glistening sharp in the cold moonbeams.
Every chamber cloaked in white,
Houses shadows, fears ignited.

Yet in the heart, a spark resides,
A flicker warm against the tides.
Through frosted walls, the spirit sings,
Of hope and life, of gentle things.

To wander here is to confront,
The bitter cold, the frozen front.
In the labyrinth, we all must roam,
Until we find our way back home.

Cascading Shadows

In tangled woods where echoes play,
Cascading shadows come to stay.
They weave between the ancient trees,
Dancing softly with the breeze.

Each footfall holds a quiet grace,
As twilight paints a secret place.
Flickers of dusk kiss the ground,
Where whispered tales are lost, then found.

Leaves drift down like gentle sighs,
Spun from dreams that never die.
The shadows stretch and blend with night,
Creating forms that catch the light.

In this realm of soft disguise,
Beneath the stars, the heart complies.
We chase the fading echoes bright,
In cascading shadows, out of sight.

Nature hums a tender tune,
As moonlight bathes the world in gloom.
We walk the paths where spirits roam,
In the shadows, we find our home.

Shivering Silhouettes

In the twilight's gentle reach,
Figures dance beneath the trees,
Whispers of the cold night speak,
Fragments of forgotten dreams.

Chilled breaths intertwine with stars,
Every shadow tells a tale,
Ghosts of warmth behind the bars,
In the silence, spirits sail.

Branches claw at fleeting light,
Hopes suspended in the air,
Lost in endless shades of night,
Shivering, they lay bare.

Footsteps crunch on frosty ground,
Echoes of a past we trace,
In this stillness, we are found,
In the dark, we find our space.

Silhouettes beneath the moon,
Waltzing in the icy haze,
Holding onto winter's tune,
As the night begins to blaze.

Enchantment in the Arctic Mist

Veils of fog caress the land,
Whispers float on frozen air,
In this realm where dreams expand,
Magic stirs without a care.

Icicles like crystal tears,
Dripping secrets from the eaves,
Every sparkle holds our fears,
In the mist, the heart believes.

Snowflakes dance on silent wings,
Weaving tales of pure delight,
Nature sings of fragile things,
In the glow of soft twilight.

Hushed enchantment fills the space,
Breath of winter, pure and bold,
In this quiet, find your grace,
Arctic dreams of white and gold.

Through the haze, the world transforms,
Landscapes change with every flake,
Where the heart in stillness warms,
Magic found in every break.

Hushed Rain of Snow

Silent falls, a gentle weight,
Patchwork quilt upon the ground,
Drifting dreams of winter's fate,
In the stillness, peace is found.

Fluttering, a world anew,
Softly wrapped in winter's grace,
Every step, a whispered hue,
In the snowy, quiet lace.

Branches heavy with the white,
Nature's beauty, pure and bright,
In this calm, our hearts take flight,
Wrapped in dreams of softest light.

Hushed rain falls, a tender gift,
Cloaking earth in frosty bliss,
In this moment, spirits lift,
Kissed by winter's icy kiss.

As the world takes breath and sleeps,
Stillness wraps the land so tight,
In the silence, beauty steep,
In the depth of longest night.

Ethereal Frosts of Silence

In the twilight's soft embrace,
Frosts of silence spread their veil,
Dreams suspended in this space,
Time flows, yet it leaves no trail.

Gentle whispers in the air,
Ethereal, the world transforms,
Nature's breath beyond compare,
In this hush, the heart conforms.

Glittering on frozen ground,
Each step echoes in the night,
In the silence, peace is found,
Stars take guardianship of light.

Branches bow beneath the weight,
Softly glistening in the glow,
Every moment, cold yet great,
In the still, we come to know.

Ethereal frost, pure delight,
Wrapping us in dreams refined,
In the depths of endless night,
Whispers of the heart entwined.

Fragments Caught in Glitter

Amidst the shards of light so bright,
Dreams scatter like stars in flight.
Each glimmer holds a tale untold,
In shadows where the past unfolds.

Whispers wrapped in silver threads,
Echoes dance where silence spreads.
Moments frozen, trapped in time,
Woven tales in rhythm and rhyme.

Textures of a world once known,
In every fragment, seeds are sown.
Memories gleam like morning dew,
Reflecting life in shades anew.

Caught in the web of dreams we chase,
Every glint a sacred place.
In fading light, the truth resides,
Where shining hope and longing hides.

So gather the fragments, weave them tight,
In the heart's embrace, they shine so bright.
For in the dark, they softly gleam,
A testament to every dream.

Frosted Veils of Memory

Veils of frost on morning's breath,
Whispers linger, a touch of death.
Each flake a memory, pure and white,
The past glistens, soft in light.

Through frozen panes, the world appears,
A silent promise, unspoken fears.
We trace the patterns, lost in thought,
Emotions trapped in battles fought.

Beneath the surface of every scene,
Lies a story, gentle and keen.
Layers of time, like frost so fine,
Embrace the heart, intertwine.

As winter wraps the world in peace,
Frosted moments will never cease.
In delicate whispers, we shall find,
The echoes of all that once was kind.

So let them dance, these veils of old,
In fragile light, their beauty bold.
For in their depths, the past holds sway,
A frosted cloak to guide our way.

The Lanterns of the Snowbound Night

In the quiet of the snowbound night,
Lanterns glow with a gentle light.
Each flicker tells a tale of old,
Warming hearts in the bitter cold.

Beneath the stars, they softly shine,
Guiding souls through the divine.
In solitude, we find our way,
With lanterns bright, we'll not delay.

In drifts of white, the paths entwine,
Each step a dance, a sacred sign.
Through frosted air, the whispers flow,
As lanterns warm the chilly glow.

They hold the dreams of those gone by,
Flickering softly, a lullaby.
In shadows deep, they share their light,
A beacon's song through the endless night.

So let the lanterns guide our fears,
Illuminating all the years.
With every flicker and every sway,
They hold the magic of our way.

Whispers in the Frosted Air

Whispers float in the frosted air,
Tender secrets, light as prayer.
In every breath, a story sown,
Between the frost, the heart is known.

The chill wraps round like a gentle hand,
In winter's embrace, we stand.
With every sigh, the world transforms,
In silent dances, the heart warms.

Echoes linger in the silver glow,
Memories traced through the soft snow.
In quiet corners, hearts reside,
With whispers soft, we confide.

Frosted dreams like lace unfold,
In the silence, stories told.
A tapestry of life we weave,
In the frosty air, we believe.

So let the whispers guide your way,
In every dawn, in every gray.
For in the chill, our spirits soar,
With whispers in the air, forevermore.

Frosted Whispers

The trees stand bare, in silence they sway,
A blanket of white, softening the day.
Whispers of frost, in the morning glow,
Nature's hush, in the crisp air flow.

Footprints linger, in the powdery bite,
Each step a story, lost to the night.
A chill in the breeze, a delicate art,
Frosted whispers, speak to the heart.

Icicles hang like crystal spears,
Reflecting the sun, through wintry years.
They shimmer and spark, in the light they dance,
Caught in the moment, a fleeting chance.

The world is still, yet alive with dreams,
In frosted whispers, nothing's as it seems.
Each breath a cloud, in the biting cold,
A tale of winter, gently told.

As dusk descends, the stars peek through,
A frosty night, a celestial view.
Wrapped in warmth, I cherish this grace,
In frosted whispers, I find my place.

Silhouettes of Winter

Against the dusk, the branches loom,
Darkened shadows, in silent gloom.
Silhouettes dance, in a moonlit trance,
Nature's display, a secret romance.

The cold winds weave, through the barren thorns,
Whispers of peace, in the early morns.
Footsteps crunch on the frosty ground,
In this quiet, solace is found.

Stars twinkle bright, like diamonds afar,
Guiding the night, where soft echoes are.
Silhouettes play, in the pale moon's glow,
A canvas of night, in winter's slow flow.

Snowflakes fall, in a delicate dance,
Each one unique, a fleeting chance.
Whispers of winter, through breezes that sigh,
In silhouettes, the world passes by.

As dawn breaks soft, the shadows retreat,
The warmth of the sun, a delicate greet.
Yet still in my heart, the silhouettes stay,
A memory woven, in winter's ballet.

Chilled Echoes

In the frozen woods, echoes ring clear,
Whispers of winter, for all who will hear.
Beneath the frost, life quietly sleeps,
Chilled echoes linger, in shadows it keeps.

The air like glass, crisp and so bright,
Each breath a cloud, in the fading light.
Footsteps imprint, a tale on the snow,
Chilled echoes tell what we may not know.

Night falls quickly, the stars take their dance,
Beneath the wide sky, we lose ourselves in chance.
Under the pale moon, secrets awake,
Chilled echoes whisper, in ripples they make.

As frost decorates the windowpane,
Nature takes pause, in a spectral chain.
The world holds its breath, in the silent hue,
Chilled echoes remind us, of dreams long overdue.

In the glow of dawn, the echoes will fade,
But the memories linger, in the stillness made.
Through the seasons' turn, they'll rise and they'll go,
Chilled echoes remain, in the heart's quiet flow.

Crystal Dreams

In a realm where silence reigns,
Crystal dreams weave through the strains.
Icicles glisten, in the morning light,
A world transformed, in pure delight.

The wind hums soft, a gentle tune,
Whispering secrets under the moon.
Snowflakes twirl, in a whimsical play,
Crystal dreams beckon, to wander away.

Amidst the pines, where shadows blend,
Nature's artistry knows no end.
Each flake a wish, from a loving heart,
In crystal dreams, we're never apart.

With every breath, the cold embraces,
Winter unfolds in delicate graces.
A tapestry spun by magical hands,
In crystal dreams, a world that expands.

As twilight whispers, the stars will ignite,
Engulfing the sky in a blanket of night.
In the hush of winter, a story redeems,
Forever held close, in our crystal dreams.

Shadows in the Snow

Softly falling, gentle white,
Whispers dance in cold moonlight.
Shadows cast on purest ground,
Silence deep, no other sound.

Footprints linger, trails so brief,
Frozen dreams, a quiet leaf.
In the stillness, secrets flow,
Nature's hush, where shadows go.

Branches bow under winter's push,
Every flake a tender hush.
Creeping dusk, the stars ignite,
Guiding spirits through the night.

Frosted breath in twilight's glow,
Whirling winds, the stories show.
In this realm of white and cold,
Magic whispers, secrets told.

Moonlit Glaciers

Silver beams on ice so grand,
Nature's craft, a sculptor's hand.
Crystal towers pierce the night,
Glistening under pale moonlight.

Echoes of the past unfold,
Frozen tales of warriors bold.
Caves of turquoise, shadows play,
Dreamlike scenes that drift away.

Serenity lies in the chill,
Silent waters, invoking still.
Reflections dance, a ghostly art,
Whispers cradle every heart.

Journey through this frozen prose,
Where the ancient glacier glows.
Underneath the stars, we roam,
In this realm, we find our home.

Tread Softly on the Ice

Step by step on the frost,
Gentle whispers, not a cost.
Softly moved, we dance around,
Nature's grace in silence found.

Cracks might beckon, ice will sigh,
Listen close, the night is nigh.
Every shiver, every sound,
Holds a mystery profound.

Footprints fading, tales erased,
Moments shared, with time embraced.
Gentle caution, hearts abide,
In this place where dreams reside.

Eyes to the horizon, bright,
Chasing shadows, chasing light.
Tread softly where spirits glide,
On the ice, let magic ride.

Glacial Mosaics

Patterns etched in purest ice,
Nature's art, a grand device.
Fragments shine in light's soft glow,
Future hints in past's tableau.

Colors burst as twilight fades,
Every shard a story laid.
Glistening fields stretch far and wide,
In the splendor, dreams reside.

Chilled reflections starry bright,
Shimmering under the night.
Together woven, old and new,
Life's own puzzle shines in view.

Echoes soft, the glacial song,
Where we all can feel we belong.
In this canvas, frost paints free,
A world of wonder, endlessly.

Shadows of a Chilling Twilight

In twilight's grasp, the shadows creep,
Silent whispers through the deep.
The world transforms in dusky grace,
As night descends, we find our space.

Frosted trees like sentinels stand,
Guarding secrets of the land.
A silver sheen on frozen ground,
In chilly air, lost dreams are found.

Stars emerge in the velvet sky,
While owls call and night birds fly.
Each gust breathes tales of the old,
In every shiver, stories told.

Menacing clouds, a subtle fright,
The chilling touch of fading light.
Yet through the dark, a promise glows,
Of dawn that soon will come and pose.

In shadows' dance, we find our peace,
A fleeting moment, sweet release.
As twilight fades, embrace the night,
For in the dark, we find the light.

The Allure of Subzero

Frigid breath, a world in blue,
Embracing all that's cold and new.
Icicles hang from eaves like teeth,
Beneath their grasp, the silence sheath.

The crystal air bites at my skin,
Yet in the chill, there's warmth within.
Snowflakes dance, a ballet divine,
Each one a note, a fleeting line.

Mountain peaks wear frosty crowns,
In stillness wrapped, the world renowns.
Nature's art, it paints so clear,
A masterpiece, both sharp and sheer.

Ghostly winds in whispers run,
Telling tales 'neath the frozen sun.
Beauty found in every flake,
In subzero's soft embrace, awake.

The allure of cold, a balm so rare,
In icy grips, we breathe the air.
Through chilling nights and glacial dreams,
Life slows down, or so it seems.

Whispering Winds of the Frozen Night

Whispers glide on frosty air,
Echoing secrets, soft as hair.
Through ancient trees, they weave and sigh,
Underneath the watchful sky.

Stars align in their distant dance,
Inviting hearts to lose a chance.
Moonlight spills on silver snow,
Enchanting eyes, a gentle glow.

Frozen branches creak and yield,
Nature's breath, a mystic shield.
Among the shadows, spirits roam,
In every gust, they call us home.

Embrace the chill, the night's caress,
In whispered winds, we find our rest.
Beneath the frost, life softly stirs,
In quietude, the magic blurs.

Together under the frozen dome,
We weave our dreams, we find our home.
In the stillness of that night,
Love's warmth becomes our guiding light.

Jaded Reflection of the Glaze

Beneath the surface, colors fade,
A jaded view through glass displayed.
Reflections twist, a fractured dream,
As frozen thoughts begin to gleam.

The world is painted in shades of gray,
Where hopes and fears both come to play.
In icy stillness, memories flow,
Trapped in time, the heartbeats slow.

Each glance a mirror, making whole,
Yet deep inside, there's yearning soul.
Through frozen glass, we seek the light,
In fleeting visions, wrong turns right.

Years whisper softly through the glaze,
In fragments lost, we wander, gaze.
Yet in the depths, a flicker shows,
The warmth of hearts, where courage grows.

So take a moment, breathe the air,
Beyond the jaded, there's a flare.
In every crack, the light shines through,
A testament to all we do.

Shattered Glass

In a room where echoes clash,
Light dances on the shards,
Memories form a fragile mask,
Each piece a thousand guards.

Reflections cut so deep,
A heart knows where to bleed,
Holding whispers, secrets seep,
From love that won't concede.

The floor is strewn with dreams,
Colorful, yet bleak they fall,
In silence, nothing seems,
To mend the shattered call.

Time can't fix what's been broke,
Yet hope flickers in the dust,
From ashes, we evoke,
A strength that turns to trust.

So gather every shard,
Fashion them into art,
In every scar, a guard,
In every piece, a heart.

Breathing in the Cold

The winter air, it bites and stings,
Each breath a foggy plume,
Amidst the trees, the silence rings,
In nature's frozen room.

Crisp snowflakes brush my cheek,
As shadows stretch and sway,
The world feels tender, soft, yet bleak,
In this unyielding gray.

Footprints echo in the night,
Leading to places lost,
In the dark, the stars ignite,
No warmth without the frost.

Whispers of the chill unwind,
The quiet holds a tune,
In icy grasp, our hearts entwined,
Beneath the silver moon.

So I breathe in the cold air,
Let it fill me to the brim,
For in this stark, desolate flair,
Hope dances on the whim.

Celestial Fragments

Stars fall from the heavens wide,
A comet's trailing grace,
Wisps of light in cosmic tide,
They vanish without trace.

Nebulas in colors bright,
Paint dreams across the skies,
Each a dance of pure delight,
Where every spark defies.

Planets spin in endless dance,
Gravity their loyal friend,
In their vast, enchanting trance,
Time, like stardust, bends.

Galaxies collide and form,
A testament to fate,
In chaos blooms a bright new norm,
Creating worlds so great.

So here beneath this cosmic dome,
I gaze, my spirit free,
In fragments, I find my home,
In stars' grand symphony.

The Frozen Gallery

In a chamber cold as night,
Art hung upon the walls,
Each frame a captured flight,
Where silence slowly calls.

Paintings frost with time's embrace,
Brush strokes whisper low,
In hues of white, they leave no trace,
Of colors long ago.

Sculptures draped in icy lace,
Figures lost in thought,
Stillness fills this sacred space,
With beauty, time forgot.

Visitors, with breath held tight,
Walk gently on the floor,
In awe of every frozen sight,
They linger, wanting more.

So I tread in hushed respect,
Through this gallery of dreams,
Where time and art connect,
In frozen, fleeting beams.

Mystique of Winter's Grip

The world wrapped in silence, so deep,
Snowflakes dance, a secret to keep.
Branches bow with the weight of the frost,
In this quiet realm, nothing is lost.

Echoes of dreams in the chilly air,
Whispers of magic, everywhere.
A shiver runs through the twilight glow,
As night falls gently, with a crystal show.

Footsteps muffled on a snowy lane,
Stories of winter, pleasure and pain.
Glistening landscapes stretch far and wide,
Inviting hearts to fall and abide.

The stars gaze down on the icy glass,
Each twinkle a wish, as moments pass.
Wrapped in warmth, we find our escape,
In winter's embrace, our souls reshape.

From rooftops, icicles hang like lace,
Nature's artwork, a stillness in grace.
The mystique of winter holds its tight grip,
As time unveils the season's soft script.

The Frost-laden Lustre

Morning breaks with a gentle gleam,
Frost-laden fields in a silvery dream.
Sunrise kisses the ground with light,
Transforming landscapes, a magical sight.

Trees wear coats of shimmering white,
Reflecting the sun, a dazzling height.
As shadows stretch and the day begins,
Lustre of frost brings warmth from within.

Birds find shelter in the quiet trees,
Chirping softly in the chilling breeze.
With every breath, they spread joy anew,
In the wonderland painted from dew.

The world awakens to winter's embrace,
Each moment cradled in delicate grace.
Under the spell of the frost-laden air,
Hearts are ignited, love's warmth to share.

As dusk descends, the chill will rise,
Stars shimmer brightly in night's reprise.
The frost-laden lustre, a beautiful song,
In the heart of winter, we find we belong.

Mirage of a Winter Dream

In a land of white where shadows blend,
A mirage appears as daylight tends.
Soft whispers of snow create a scene,
A vision of wonder, tranquil and serene.

Drifting clouds of a delicate hue,
Paint the horizon with the softest blue.
Nature's brilliance in silence unfolds,
As miracles form in the bitter cold.

Frosted crystals light up the night,
Glimmers of diamonds, a wondrous sight.
Each step taken leaves a trace,
In the mirage of winter, we find our place.

Voices carry on the brisk, cool air,
Promises made with a tender care.
In this fleeting moment, dreams take flight,
As hearts awaken to the magic of night.

With every breath, a tale to weave,
Whispers of warmth beneath the eave.
In the mirage where shadows gleam,
We dance through the fabric of winter's dream.

Crystalline Nightfall

As daylight wanes and shadows creep,
Winter's night calls us into her deep.
A tapestry woven of stars and frost,
In crystalline nightfall, no moment's lost.

The moon hangs low, a guardian bright,
Casting soft beams in the velvety night.
Trees shimmer gently in silvery sheens,
Wrapped in the beauty of frozen scenes.

An ethereal hush blankets the earth,
In this quiet hour, we find rebirth.
Every flake a wish, gently spun,
As night unfolds, new dreams have begun.

Crystals twinkle in the heavens' glow,
Weaving their magic in a dance slow.
This world bathed in calm brings peace to the soul,
In crystalline nightfall, we feel whole.

Hearts intertwine in the chill of the air,
Warmth of togetherness, a precious flare.
Beneath this quilt of twinkling light,
We gather close on a winter's night.

Luminescent Paths of Winter

In the hush of falling snow,
Footprints whisper soft and slow.
Moonlight dances on the ground,
Where secrets of the night are found.

Branches glisten, cloaked in white,
Stars above, a twinkling sight.
Each breath hangs like misty lace,
A tranquil calm, a hushed embrace.

Crystal shadows blend and sway,
Guiding travelers on their way.
Through the woods, so still and deep,
Winter's magic softly creeps.

Fires flicker in the dark,
Warmth ignites a gentle spark.
Voices echo, tales retold,
Of journeys shared in the cold.

As dawn breaks with gentle light,
The world awakes, a splendid sight.
Paths of silver, glints, and gleam,
Winter holds a fragile dream.

Dance of the Shimmering Frost

Frost-kissed mornings greet the dawn,
Nature's veil, a mystic fawn.
Each crystal breathes a tale of old,
In the chill, a warmth unfolds.

Underneath a sky so bright,
Snowflakes twirl, a pure delight.
Branches bow in silent grace,
As the world finds its embrace.

Whispering winds carry tales far,
Echoing dreams beneath the star.
The dance of frost, a fleeting chance,
Under the moon, a frozen dance.

Footsteps crunch on icy trails,
Resonating like sweet gales.
In the stillness, life ignites,
With shimmering frost in dazzling sights.

As twilight wraps the day in gold,
Worn hearts gather 'round the bold.
With laughter's warmth against the chill,
Winter's dance is ours to fill.

A Lament in Crystal

In the silence of the frost,
Whispers speak of all we've lost.
Time encased in icy tears,
Echoing our long-held fears.

Each flake falls with heavy heart,
A crystalline work of art.
Memories etched in snow and ice,
A delicate, haunting price.

Through the night, shadows creep,
Secrets buried, buried deep.
In the cold, they find their voice,
A lament we dare not choice.

Stars above, with sorrow gleam,
Lighting up the frozen dream.
Holding tight to what we grieve,
As winter's grasp will not leave.

Yet in the chill, hope can bloom,
As dawn breaks and shadows loom.
A soft promise, bright and clear,
In winter's heart, love draws near.

The Grasp of True Cold

Bitter winds that cut the face,
Each breath freezes in its place.
Winter brings its stern embrace,
A world transformed, time suspended in grace.

The branches crack beneath the weight,
Of white, as if to contemplate.
Shivers dance down every spine,
Beneath the vast and frosty line.

In this hush, the world feels small,
Echoes of life, a muted call.
A tapestry of frost unfolds,
Woven stories, whispers bold.

Yet beneath that icy breath,
Lies the warmth, a promise of life, not death.
For in the cold, hearts learn to be,
Resilient as the tallest tree.

With every harsh and freezing night,
Comes the dawn, the return of light.
The cycle spins, as shadows fade,
In winter's grasp, our strength displayed.

Glimmering Abyss

In the depths where shadows dwell,
A luminescent tale to tell.
Whispers lost in velvet night,
Glimmers spark, a fleeting light.

Waves of darkness, calm and cold,
Secrets from the deep unfold.
Echoes linger, soft and low,
In the abyss, dreams softly flow.

Drifting thoughts like starry dust,
In the silence, find your trust.
Gazing deep, the soul's embrace,
In the glimmering, find your place.

Voices call from realms unseen,
In the heart where fears have been.
Shadows dance, then fade away,
In this abyss, night meets day.

Yet within the dark resides,
Hope that glimmers, love abides.
Through the void, a journey wide,
In the abyss, we confide.

Shades of the Polar Night

In the stillness, cold winds sigh,
Underneath the darkened sky.
Stars like whispers, soft and low,
Guide the way where spirits go.

Draped in shadows, wild and free,
Embers of eternity.
Frosty breath in silver shades,
Night unfolds as daylight fades.

Colors shift in frozen air,
Dreams unspool, a world laid bare.
In the quiet, hearts ignite,
Finding warmth in polar night.

Echoes dance of ancient lore,
Across the ice, through every door.
Silent songs, the past recalls,
In the night, our spirit calls.

Through the glaze of purest white,
Nature's heart begins to fight.
Underneath the dreamy skies,
Shades of night, where wisdom lies.

Glacial Music

Melodies of ice entwine,
Nature's song, pure and divine.
Crisp and clear, the notes arise,
Whispers of the winter skies.

Glacial chords like crystals break,
In a stillness, echoes wake.
Every flake has tales to share,
A harmony beyond compare.

With each gust, the rhythm flows,
Crackling sounds, the silence grows.
Frozen rivers hum along,
In the chill, the heart finds song.

Beneath the frost, a pulse exists,
In the dance of nature's tryst.
Fortunes fold in icy glades,
In this music, life cascades.

Notes like stars begin to shine,
In the night, we intertwine.
Glacial echoes softly play,
Guiding us along the way.

The Dance of Frost

Frosty tendrils weave and spin,
In the quiet, life begins.
Glistening in the morning light,
Nature's dancers, pure and bright.

Twisting patterns in the air,
Every shimmer, a silent prayer.
Branches clothed in icy lace,
Celebrating winter's grace.

Underneath the silver sheen,
Life's reflections, seldom seen.
In this dance, the world will sway,
To the rhythm of the day.

Snowflakes twirl, a ballet grand,
Across the hills, a white expanse.
With each step, the chill invites,
A frosty waltz beneath moonlight.

As the dusk begins to fall,
Frosty whispers softly call.
In the night, the shadows play,
The dance of frost, a bright display.

Specters in the Cold

In shadows where the frost takes hold,
Whispers linger in the night,
Figures dance, both shy and bold,
Veils of winter, pale and white.

Echoes drift on icy breath,
Footsteps falter, lost in time,
The chill embraces life and death,
In silence, secrets softly rhyme.

Glimmers fade like distant stars,
Hushed by frost's relentless plea,
Between the trees and frozen bars,
Specters roam, wild and free.

Beneath the moon's unwavering gaze,
Shadows weave their ancient lore,
Through the night, a spectral haze,
Fingers brush the forgotten door.

With every breath, the cold distinct,
Stories linger in the air,
In the void, connections linked,
A haunting beauty, rich and rare.

Whispering Chill

A whisper lingers on the breeze,
Carried through the snowy night,
Fractured hopes beneath the trees,
Dreams wrapped tight in silver light.

The chill seeps deep into the ground,
Crystals form on trembling leaves,
Mysteries in silence found,
Time stands still, as nature heaves.

Frosted breath of twilight's song,
Calls from shadows, soft and near,
In the depths where echoes throng,
Every moment fraught with fear.

A dance of light, the shadows play,
In gardens cloaked beneath the frost,
Where memories of warmth decay,
And voices list, in dreams embossed.

Yet in this chill, a warmth resides,
A gentle pulse, a heart's refrain,
In whispers wrapped, where hope abides,
The songs of winter, sweet yet plain.

The Ethereal Tranquility

In stillness wrapped in silver sheen,
The world rests soft beneath the sky,
A canvas of ethereal green,
Where calm and chaos glide on by.

Mist embraces the hollow trees,
Crimson leaves drift to the ground,
The quiet hum of winter's breeze,
A tranquil space where dreams are found.

Stars emerge in silent prayer,
Their twinkle whispers in the night,
With every moment, cool and rare,
Awakening the heart's delight.

Lightly dances the evening glow,
Painting shadows upon the glade,
In the embrace of falling snow,
Every sigh in stillness laid.

Beneath the sky of twilight's hue,
Where whispers weave through icy air,
A promise held in every view,
A world of peace, beyond compare.

A Breath of Frost

A breath of frost, so delicate,
Wraps the earth in a subtle veil,
In winter's grasp, we contemplate,
The fleeting warmth, a secret tale.

Wind caresses the crystal streams,
In silence sings a fleeting song,
Reflections caught in frigid dreams,
Where everything feels right yet wrong.

The stars above, like diamonds bright,
Whisper truths in the cooling air,
As shadows meld into the night,
A world enchanted, rich and rare.

Each breath that clouds, a moment lost,
In frozen time, sensations blend,
A fragile touch, a gentle frost,
A striking bond, a lover's end.

In every chill, a spark ignites,
In stillness, hearts are drawn anew,
Embracing tales of winter's nights,
As we find warmth in waters blue.

Veils of the Arctic

Whispers of snow in the frigid air,
Veils of white drape the tundra bare.
Under the moon, a silver glow,
Nature's canvas, a spectral show.

Glaciers shimmer in twilight's embrace,
Chasing shadows, they dance with grace.
Cold winds howl through jagged peaks,
Secrets the icy silence keeps.

Beneath the frost, the earth takes breath,
Life persists in the chill of death.
Footprints trace where few have dared,
In the quiet, beauty shared.

Auroras blaze in hues so bright,
Painting the dark with ethereal light.
A realm untouched by the hands of man,
In this vast hush, mysteries span.

Frozen realms, a world apart,
Echoes of nature's beating heart.
Through veils of ice, we glimpse the soul,
In Arctic beauty, we find our whole.

Luminous Transparency

Ice crystals sparkle, capturing the sun,
Each fragment tells of battles won.
In purest form, the world is seen,
Through luminous layers, vibrant, keen.

Beneath the surface, stories hide,
Of ancient seas and the tides that bide.
Transparency grants us fleeting sight,
Of all that lives in the cold, pale light.

Winds whisper secrets through frosted trees,
Floating dreams on a gentle breeze.
Fractured colors, a sight divine,
Reflections dance, in glass they twine.

Each crystal holds a memory dear,
Of seasons shifting year by year.
With every thaw, a tale unfolds,
Of nature's wonders and truths retold.

In this realm of clarity and grace,
We seek the warmth of time and space.
Luminous beauty, an endless chase,
Through translucent dreams, we find our place.

Frigid Footprints

In the blanket of snow, footprints appear,
Whispers of journeys we hold dear.
Shapes in the frost tell stories untold,
Of travelers brave, both young and old.

Each step reveals a moment's trace,
Captured in winter's tender embrace.
Across the field where shadows sleep,
Frigid paths where secrets creep.

Time pauses here in the snowy expanse,
Echoes of life in a frozen dance.
Frozen paths lead us to explore,
The hidden wonders, the open door.

Oceans of white stretch far and wide,
In this cold realm, we cast aside.
Frigid footprints lead to the unknown,
In every stride, a story sown.

In the silence, we find our quest,
Seeking answers, we are blessed.
Beneath the stars, our spirits rise,
In the cold night, the world belies.

Enigmas of the Freeze

In twilight hours, the chill descends,
Mysteries hide where the cold wind bends.
Frosted whispers, a cryptic song,
A world of wonders where we belong.

Shapes shift beneath a snowy veil,
Frozen secrets in the milky pale.
Nature's riddle in ice and snow,
In every crack, the stories flow.

Depths conceal what sight can't glean,
Life endures in the winter's sheen.
Beneath the frost, the heart remains,
In enigmas, beauty reigns.

Crystals form in the quiet night,
Glistening softly in pale moonlight.
Each glimmer holds a truth so bright,
Shadows dance in the cold twilight.

In stillness, we ponder the freeze,
The depth of silence, the breath of trees.
With every glance, new worlds arise,
In frozen realms, the soul complies.

Beneath the Frosted Canopy

Under branches heavy with snow,
Whispers of silence softly flow.
The world is wrapped in a white embrace,
Nature holds a still, secret space.

Footprints left in powdery trails,
Echo the stories of winter's tales.
Each breath visible, a cloud of dreams,
Beneath the canopy, nothing is as it seems.

Frosted bits twinkle like stars,
A canvas of white, adorned with scars.
Hope lingers in the crisp, cold air,
Magic weaves through with gentle care.

Veils of ice hang down from the trees,
Shimmering softly with each passing breeze.
Winter's breath on the frozen land,
Crafts an art that is grand and planned.

In this realm of the cold and bright,
Every shadow holds a sliver of light.
Here in the stillness, the heart feels free,
Beneath the frosted canopy.

The Soft Glance of Winter

Morning breaks with a gentle sigh,
Softly painted in hues of sky.
Snowflakes dance in the pale light,
Winter's touch, ever so slight.

Each tree dressed in a silvery gown,
Nature's beauty, a jewel crown.
Chill in the air, refreshing and clear,
Embraced by the season, we draw near.

Footsteps crunch on the frozen ground,
Echoes of peace in the quiet found.
In this moment, time feels slow,
The soft glance of winter, a lovely show.

Above, the clouds are soft and gray,
Yet in the stillness, hope finds its way.
A promise whispered in the chill,
Winter's charm, a potion to fill.

As day turns to dusk, the glow ignites,
Stars appear, piercing the nights.
Wrapped in warmth, a cozy delight,
We linger longer in winter's sight.

Haunting Chills in the Stillness

In the heart of the night, shadows grow,
A whispering breeze begins to flow.
Haunting chills creep through the air,
As if the world holds its breath in prayer.

Branches sway with a ghostly grace,
In the dark, there's a familiar face.
Silence echoes, a haunting tune,
In the stillness beneath the moon.

Footsteps barely make a sound,
Yet memories linger, profound.
Each star a witness in the deep,
To secrets that the night will keep.

Frosted windows dimly glow,
Hints of warmth where it's safe to go.
Yet outside, the chill speaks clear,
Of stories buried deep in fear.

As dawn creeps in, the chill will wane,
But echoes of night still remain.
In every heart, a tender thrill,
From haunting chills in the stillness, instill.

Crystal Grasp of the Night

Night descends with a quiet force,
Wrapped in secrets, a powerful course.
Stars scatter like diamonds up high,
In the crystal grasp of the night sky.

Moonlight spills on the frozen ground,
Transforming the world without a sound.
Whispers of dreams drift through the trees,
In this silence, hearts find ease.

Ripples of frost paint the air,
Reflecting magic, everywhere.
Each breath a moment, pure and bright,
Captured in the crystal grasp of night.

Time seems to pause in the cool embrace,
As shadows blend, creating space.
A dance of light in a world so wide,
Guided by the moon, a trusted guide.

As the night deepens, we feel its call,
A canopy of wonders to enthrall.
In the stillness, let your spirit take flight,
Embrace the magic of the night so bright.

Frozen Dancers

In the silence of the night,
Figures twirl in purest white,
Graceful moves in icy air,
Enchanting dreams, a world so rare.

Underneath the silver glow,
Whispers travel soft and slow,
Every glide, a story told,
In a dance both brave and bold.

Frosty breath upon their cheeks,
Glittering tales the winter seeks,
Footprints trace the frozen ground,
Where hidden magic can be found.

Stars align, the moon ascends,
Frozen hearts that time suspends,
Held together through the chill,
Where winter's beauty haunts us still.

As dawn breaks with gentle light,
Dancing shadows take their flight,
In the dawn, forever pranced,
The heart of winter, tightly danced.

The Hushed Breath of December

Beneath a cloak of gentle snow,
Forests hum a tranquil show,
Branches draped with icy lace,
Nature wears a quiet face.

Every step, a muffled sound,
In this stillness, peace is found,
Time stands still as frost appears,
Whispers shared through silent years.

Sparking lights in windows glow,
Inviting warmth, a soft hello,
Candles flicker, shadows play,
In December's gentle sway.

Frosted breath like tender sighs,
Underneath the clouded skies,
Hearts entwined in whispered prayer,
Love and hope are everywhere.

With each flake that drifts down low,
A promise wrapped in winter's glow,
In this hush, the world will rest,
Finding peace, our hearts confessed.

Shards of a Frigid Dawn

Piercing light through frosty panes,
Awakens dreams where silence reigns,
Windows glimmer, shards of gold,
As winter's breath begins to fold.

Morning breaks with whispered glee,
Chasing night toward the sea,
Ice and gleam in vibrant play,
Waking life, dispelling grey.

Each crystal formed in night's embrace,
Reflects the beauty of this place,
Promises in every beam,
Awakening the heart's soft dream.

A tapestry of light unfolds,
In every hue, the story told,
Frosty air, the world adorned,
As dawn's embrace leaves us transformed.

So let the day be born anew,
With every shard that dances through,
In the stillness of the morn,
We find the warmth of dreams reborn.

Luminous Fragments of Cold

Glistening stars in midnight sky,
Breathe the whispers of goodbye,
Each flake, a diamond's light,
Falling softly through the night.

Shattered pieces, pure and bright,
Form a canvas, cold delight,
Crisp and clear, the world awakes,
In the stillness, magic breaks.

Gentle glow of morning sun,
Shining where the shadows run,
Cold embrace, a tender touch,
Filling hearts that yearn so much.

Every moment, time stands still,
In this dance of winter's chill,
Luminous fragments all around,
In this wonder, joy is found.

So let us cherish winter's gift,
A chance for hearts and spirits to lift,
With every sparkle in the cold,
A warmth within, a story told.

Secrets in the Frozen Grove

Whispers linger in the trees,
Branches heavy, chilled by freeze.
Snowflakes twirl like thoughts untold,
Cradling secrets, bright and cold.

Footsteps crunch on frosted ground,
In the quiet, peace is found.
Frozen whispers dance in air,
Silent tales of winter's care.

Shadows stretch where sunlight plays,
Hiding truths in winter's haze.
Glimmers spark in every glade,
Nature's art, a soft cascade.

In this grove, the heartbeats blend,
Echoes of the trees, our friends.
Every sigh and gentle breeze,
Carries whispers through the leaves.

Secrets linger, smooth like ice,
Waiting still, a rare device.
Listen close, let nature speak,
In the frozen grove, seek the peak.

Echos of a Winter's Breath

In the stillness of the night,
Winter's breath, a fleeting light.
Echoes whisper through the air,
Carrying dreams beyond compare.

Silver frost on every leaf,
Crystals weave in nature's brief.
Softly glows the moon above,
Bathing all in frosty love.

Each exhale, a tale retold,
Directions veiled in purest gold.
Listen closely, hear the sound,
Of winter's heart that holds its ground.

Frozen rivers, glistening bright,
Reflections dance in pale moonlight.
A world transformed, serene and clear,
Embracing all that draws us near.

Whispers echo, soft and deep,
In the night where shadows sleep.
Echos of a life once known,
Winter's breath, in frost, has grown.

Twilight's Icy Embrace

Twilight falls on snowy ground,
Where silence wraps the world around.
An icy breath upon my face,
Invites me to this frozen space.

Shadows blend, the day must yield,
To a night where dreams are sealed.
Stars emerge, like diamonds bright,
Casting wishes into the night.

Frosted whispers softly sing,
Of ancient tales the night can bring.
In twilight's hush, I find my peace,
As winter's magic offers release.

Here in frost, the heart beats slow,
In the still, where feelings grow.
Twilight wraps the world in grace,
As the stars find their rightful place.

Beneath the frost, the earth does sleep,
In icy arms, secrets I keep.
Twilight's touch, a gentle trace,
Forever holds, in its embrace.

Fragments of Frosted Light

In the morning's soft embrace,
Frosted light begins to grace.
Every crystal, a gentle gleam,
Dancing bright, like a waking dream.

Sunrise kisses the world anew,
Painting skies with shades of blue.
Whispers of warmth in the air,
Fleeting moments, moments rare.

Through the branches, shadows play,
Chasing night, welcoming day.
Fragments spark, a bright parade,
Nature's artwork, never fade.

Glistening paths that beckon near,
Every step, the heart can hear.
Footprints trailing in the snow,
Leaving stories where we go.

Hope and wonder fill the scene,
In this universe, so serene.
Fragments of light, a soft caress,
In each moment, we are blessed.

Echoes of a Bitter Breeze

In the stillness of the night,
Whispers carry, taking flight.
Chilling tales from far away,
Stories frozen, hearts in sway.

The trees creak in solemn grace,
Nature's voice, a haunted place.
Ghostly winds through branches weep,
Echoes in the dark, they creep.

Bitter gusts, they weave and wail,
Tales of sorrow, hearts that pale.
Frigid breath upon my skin,
Lingers as the night wears thin.

Footsteps crunch on icy ground,
Memories of warmth, unbound.
Fleeting warmth, a distant glow,
In the breeze, a tale of woe.

Echoes fade, but still they cling,
In the heart, the silence sings.
Bitter breeze, your song I'll keep,
In my dreams, where shadows sleep.

Twinkling Snowbound Lullabies

Snowflakes dance on winter's breath,
Whispers soft as dreams of rest.
A blanket white, the world in peace,
In this calm, all worries cease.

Stars adorn the midnight sky,
Twinkling gems as time slips by.
Hushed beneath the silver haze,
Nighttime's soft and gentle gaze.

Crystals shimmer, stories told,
Lullabies in the moonlight's hold.
Each flake falls with tender grace,
Wrapping secrets in their embrace.

Hearts awake to silence pure,
In this midst, we feel the cure.
Nature's song, a soothing balm,
In winter's glow, we find our calm.

Snowbound dreams embrace the night,
Wrapped in warmth, we feel the light.
Quiet whispers, soft and low,
In this stillness, love will grow.

The Enigma of Frost

Frosted windows, morning's sheen,
Nature's artwork, crisp and clean.
Mysteries in patterns bright,
Delicate truths, hidden from sight.

Each breath hangs in the air
Whispers of beauty, cold and rare.
The world transforms, a silent art,
Frost embraces every part.

Lace-like wonders, fleeting shows,
In frozen moments, magic flows.
Secrets held in icy frames,
Life's reflections, without names.

Awake the senses, see the light,
Glistening crystals, pure delight.
Frost speaks softly, hidden lore,
In its silence, we explore.

The enigma, a gentle grasp,
Nature's touch, an icy clasp.
Frost will fade with morning's sun,
Yet in our hearts, the chill will run.

Moonlight's Silent Caress

Moonlight spills on soft, cool ground,
Washing over all around.
Softly kissed by silver beams,
In this glow, we hold our dreams.

The night unfolds, a gentle sigh,
Whispers float like stars on high.
In the hush, our thoughts take flight,
Dancing shadows, lost in light.

Through the leaves, the soft glow weaves,
Nature hums in quiet eaves.
Silent caress, a lover's touch,
Moonlit secrets that mean so much.

Each moment feels both strange and clear,
In moon's embrace, we feel no fear.
Time slows down and whispers sweet,
In this light, our hearts will meet.

Moonlight fades, yet echoes stay,
In our hearts, the light will play.
Silent caress that lingers long,
In remembered dreams, we find our song.

Luminous Frost

In the quiet of the dawn,
Crystals twinkle like stars,
Frozen breath in the air,
Nature's art, on our behalf.

Branches draped in white silk,
Each flake tells a story,
A dance of soft silence,
The world wrapped in glory.

Footsteps echo on frozen ground,
Whispers of dreams below,
While shadows stretch and yawn,
As daybreak starts to glow.

Light glimmers in the chill,
Painting shadows long and bright,
Moments snatched from time,
As day surrenders to night.

The spell of winter's grace,
Encased in frost's embrace,
Each breath a frost-laced word,
In this soft, frozen place.

The Soft Cradle of Winter

In the hush of falling snow,
Nature sleeps, soft and slow,
Gentle whispers fill the air,
A tender, frosty care.

Blankets thick of purest white,
Cradle dreams through silent nights,
Stars above begin to wink,
In this peace, we softly sink.

The world is wrapped in twilight,
Every branch gleams with delight,
Crisp and clear, the air so still,
Winter's heart, a boundless thrill.

Time is woven through the cold,
Secret stories yet untold,
In each flake, a tale of old,
Memories wrapped in white gold.

The soft cradle holds us close,
In its arms, we learn the most,
With every breath, snowflakes twine,
A world that feels just divine.

Bound by Frost

Underneath a silver moon,
Crystaled paths invite a tune,
Footfalls light and spirits high,
The earth dressed in winter's sigh.

Shadows dance on icy streams,
Where nature whispers secret dreams,
Every heartbeat, every breath,
A solitary song of death.

Moonbeams kiss the frozen ground,
Echoes of a world profound,
Branch and bough with frosted lace,
Nature moves at a sacred pace.

In the hush, all worries fade,
Moments of joy softly laid,
Bound by frost, we find our way,
In winter's arms, we choose to stay.

Stars above weave tales unknown,
In this chilly realm, we've grown,
Each breath a promise sweetly sought,
In frost, our solace finely caught.

A Charmed Cusp of Cold

On the edge of winter's breath,
Where silence sprinkles life and death,
A tapestry of white and gray,
The cusp of cold begins to play.

Glistening waves of icy flair,
Wrap the world in wintry stare,
Each morning brings a crisp delight,
As dawn thaws away the night.

Palms pressed warm against the pane,
We watch the dance of snow and rain,
Whirling shadows wild and free,
A charmed cusp, just you and me.

Time, it seems, has gently paused,
In these moments, we're not lost,
Nature sings her frosty hymn,
As we bask at winter's rim.

A spellbound realm of glimmering light,
Invites us into the wintry night,
In every flake, a secret told,
In this heart, we'll never grow cold.

Milton Keynes UK
Ingram Content Group UK Ltd.
UKHW010229111224
452348UK00011B/619